It's fun to pass the time away
By swinging on a sunny day
Or going on a picnic, too—
I don't know which is best, do you?

Down by the Sea

WE love the sea on a holiday
When we can be outdoors and play,
Building castles in the sand—
Don't they look so fine and grand!

Soon the tide comes rushing in
And covers where our castle's been,
Then we go bathing hand in hand—
You can't do that upon dry land!

But some don't want a sandy shore,
They like the fields and forest more—
And beautiful though that may be,
We certainly prefer the sea!

At times we think it's fun to fly
A kite in a windy summer sky,
But other times, we'd rather blow
Great big bubbles to and fro!

Apple Picking

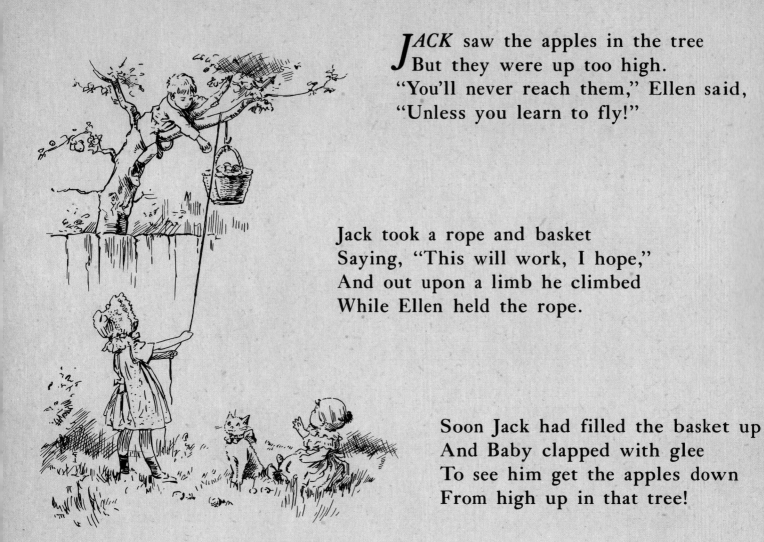

*J*ACK saw the apples in the tree
But they were up too high.
"You'll never reach them," Ellen said,
"Unless you learn to fly!"

Jack took a rope and basket
Saying, "This will work, I hope,"
And out upon a limb he climbed
While Ellen held the rope.

Soon Jack had filled the basket up
And Baby clapped with glee
To see him get the apples down
From high up in that tree!

It makes us smile to climb and play
Around the countryside all day,
But even when we're back in town
There's no need to wear a frown!

Neddy

*N*EDDY, the little donkey, said,
"Though I am only small,
I'm just as careful as can be
And won't let baby fall.

"Giving little children rides
Is what I like to do,
I love them all so very much—
And know they love *me* too!

"So maybe when it's summertime
And we're all by the sea,
Instead of riding sister Jane,
Baby can ride on me!"

Be sure there's someone at your side
   So you're not stranded by high tide,
And gathering seaweed, as you know,
Is safest when the tide is low.

Polly's Speech

*P*OLLY made a speech one day
   Talking in her squawky way—
The children listened in surprise,
They didn't know she was so wise!

"Everyone you ever met
Has had some sort of special pet,
And that is just as it should be,"
Wise Polly said, "—you both have *me!*"

Then the children asked in fun,
"Why Polly dear, do you have one?"
"Oh-ho," said Polly, "I have two—
Right before me; *you* and *you!*"

Pretty Polly likes to eat
   A lump of sugar for a treat—
But to a bunny, cute and small,
That wouldn't be a treat at all!

Out in the Country

O^{UT} in the country Jenny goes!
  There's a gentle breeze that blows,
There the grass is soft and green
Like a carpet for a queen.

She can fly a big balloon
In the sky all afternoon—
Don't forget to hold on tight
Or it will sail right out of sight!

Jenny loves to play out there
Breathing flower-scented air,
Hearing little birds in song—
She is happy all day long.